# track & field's
## new wave

# Marion
# Jones

*Fast and Fearless*

## BY
## RACHEL RUTLEDGE

THE MILLBROOK PRESS
BROOKFIELD, CONNECTICUT

THE MILLBROOK PRESS

Produced by
BITTERSWEET PUBLISHING
John Sammis, President
and
TEAM STEWART, INC.

Series Design and Electronic Page Makeup by
JAFFE ENTERPRISES
Ron Jaffe

Researched and Edited by Mark Stewart

All photos courtesy
AP/ Wide World Photos, Inc. except the following:
The Sporting News: Kirby Lee, photographer — Cover
Los Angeles Daily News — Pages 7, 9, 14, 15, 16
University of North Carolina — Pages 17, 19, 22, 23, 24, 26
The following images are from the collection of Team Stewart:
ACOG (© 1992) — Page 10
Sports Illustrated (© 1991) — Page 25
Runner's World/Rodale Press (© 1998) — Page 37
Editions Rencontre S.A. (© 1977) — Page 38 (bottom, right
Classic Games Inc. (© 1992) — Page 40
ESPN Inc. (© 2000) — Page 47



Printed in the United States of America

Published by
The Millbrook Press, Inc.
2 Old New Milford Road
Brookfield, Connecticut 06804

www.millbrookpress.com

Library of Congress Cataloging-in-Publication Data

Rutledge, Rachel.
Marion Jones: fast and fearless / by Rachel Rutledge.
p.cm. – (Track & field's new wave)
Includes index.
ISBN 0-7613-1870-4 (lib. bdg)
1. Jones, Marion, 1975–Juvenile literature. 2. Runners (Sports)–United States–Biography–Juvenile literature. 3. Women runners–United States–Biography–Juvenile literature. [1. Jones, Marion, 1975–2. Track and field athletes. 3. Women–Biography. 4. Afro-Americans–Biography.] I. Title. II. Series.

GV1061.15.J67 R87 2000
796.42′2′092–dc21
[B] 00-030514

1 3 5 7 9 10 8 6 4 2

# Contents

# From Dominance To Despair

chapter 1

*"Ira was always there for my sister...then he was gone."*

**— MARION'S BROTHER, ALBERT**

Some athletes are fueled by anger. Others are inspired by love. In her remarkable career as a basketball player and track star, Marion Jones has used both—often at the very same time. Strong, independent, and gifted, with a great mind and tremendous body, she has followed her unique path to stardom.

Marion's mother, whose name also is Marion, came to the United States in 1968, at the age of 22, from the Central American country of Belize. She was married briefly, had a son (Marion's older brother, Albert Kelly), then divorced. She moved to California in 1971 and married George Jones, Marion's father. Marion was born in Los Angeles in 1975. George left the family when his daughter was very young. He continued to live nearby, in Los Angeles, where he owns a laundromat. But he has had almost no contact with Marion since he left. To this day, Marion does not know or understand why.

*Twists, turns, and tragedies have marked Marion's life from the very beginning. Through it all, she has managed to stay focused and relaxed.*

*The children of Belize consider Marion one of their own, even though she was born in the United States. Because her mother was born in the Central American country, Marion holds dual citizenship.*

In 1983, Marion's mother moved the family out of Los Angeles, to the quiet town of Palmdale. There she met Ira Toler, who became her third husband. Ira was a great stepfather. While Marion's mother worked long hours as a transcriptionist (typing the recorded notes of doctors and lawyers), Ira stayed home and took care of the kids. That meant he was Marion's coach, trainer, and driver during the time she was discovering her great talent for sports. As a result, the two became extremely close.

Marion was a tough little kid. In fact, the other children called her "Hard Nails." When she set her mind to something, there was no way to talk her out of it. She did not like to play with other girls, so she hung around with Albert and his friends. At first, they did not want to let her play in their games—she seemed too young and too small. Soon they were *afraid* to let her play. Marion was faster, stronger, and more coordinated than they were!

Whatever sport Marion tried, she quickly mastered, from T-ball to soccer to gymnastics. She even excelled at ballet. By the time she was nine, Albert had introduced her to pee-wee track, and her name was beginning to appear in the local sports pages. At 10, Marion was national champion for her age group. Meanwhile, she also was the star of the Palmdale Little League. All she had to do was lay her bat on the ball and just

**Did You Know?**

As a child, Marion developed such tremendous upper-body strength and balance in gymnastics that she could walk several hundred yards on her hands.

outrun the throw to first. If one of her hits found its way into the outfield, she was around the bases in a flash.

Life seemed perfect to Marion. She felt she could achieve anything. Then the horrible news came: Ira had suffered a massive heart attack. He was dead.

Marion blows away the competition in a high-school race.
She won her first national championship as a fifth grader.

# chapter 1

# Moving Around

> *"I was very young*
> *and inexperienced."*
> — **MARION JONES**

arion was devastated by her stepfather's death. Her mother, also heartbroken, feared the family would fall apart without Ira to hold it together. Realizing Marion had a great future in sports, she encouraged her daughter to become a world-class athlete. It would give her goals and take her mind off the tragedy.

Marion Toler knew her daughter would not reach her potential in a remote area like Palmdale—the family had to move closer to Los Angeles. Big Marion, Little Marion, and Albert found a small apartment in Sherman Oaks, an affluent suburb north of Los Angeles, in the sports-crazy San Fernando Valley. The family selected Sherman Oaks because its junior high school, Pinecrest, had an excellent athletic program. Marion flourished at Pinecrest with better competition and coaching, and began developing her talent for sprinting.

*Marion loosens up on the track at Rio Mesa High School in 1990.*
*It was at Rio Mesa that she also became a top basketball player.*

*Wilma Rudolph, who won three gold medals in 1960, was honored with her own Olympic trading card 32 years later. As a teenager, Marion reminded a lot of people of Rudolph, who never lost a race in high school.*

Marion was a natural. She exploded out of the starting blocks and then just kept going faster. She won many races by yards instead of inches. When Marion was 13, she got the thrill of her life. She was introduced to Jackie Joyner-Kersee, one of history's greatest all-around athletes and Marion's all-time hero. "I got to shake Jackie's hand," she remembers. "I don't think I washed my hands for weeks."

When Marion was ready for high school, the family moved again, to the nearby town of Camarillo. She attended Rio Mesa High School and became the star of the track team. When Marion began to show great talent in basketball (she had taken up the game as a 7th Grader), her mother moved the family again, to Thousand Oaks, which had good track and basketball programs. Soon Marion was a national celebrity. During the spring of 1991, she recorded the fastest times of any high-schooler in the 100, 200, and 400 meters. This performance led to an appearance on ABC-TV's *Good Morning America*.

That spring, Marion was invited to compete at the U.S. Track & Field Championships. She watched every move the sport's superstars made, how athletes like Jackie Joyner-Kersee and Carl Lewis handled themselves during warm-ups and in front of the press. She noticed how the other competitors looked at these great athletes and realized that there was a lot of psychology to com-

## Did You Know?

Thousand Oaks went 60-4 during Marion's two seasons with the basketball team, and climbed to #8 in the national polls.

petition. It is much easier to beat someone who expects to lose, she saw. From that day on, Marion always tried to intimidate her rivals.

Meanwhile, Marion's basketball was becoming pretty intimidating. She used her quickness to smother opponents on defense, and her raw speed to burst out on the fast break. Marion's shooting and ball-handling skills were exceptional for a player her age, especially one who played forward. And she was a rebounding powerhouse. By the time she turned 16, Marion—who stood two inches short of six feet—could leap high enough to touch the rim. She was one of the top schoolgirl ballplayers in the country.

Despite Little Marion's basketball exploits, Big Marion believed her future lay in track. In 1992, after Marion obliterated the high-school record for the 200 meters, her mother talked Elliott Mason into giving Marion special training. Despite her daughter's age, she thought Marion could make the Olympic team headed for Barcelona, Spain, that summer. Mason, who had once coached Evelyn Ashford (one of America's most successful sprinters) agreed.

Mason helped refine Marion's sprinting technique, making small adjustments in the way she carried her arms and positioned her head. Mason explained that against the likes of international superstars Gail Devers, Inger Miller, and Gwen Torrence, a tenth of a second could make the difference between making the national team and watching the Olympics on TV.

*From observing Olympic gold medalist Jackie Joyner-Kersee, Marion learned the importance of intimidating her rivals.*

# Not As Easy As It Looks!

*Since her grade-school days, people have always said Marion makes sprinting look easy. Marion claims they are wrong. "They don't see the injuries," she says. "They don't see all the mornings I'm up at seven lifting weights. They don't see all the frustrations."*

In the spring of 1992, Marion attended the Olympic trials. She needed to finish in the top three in the 100 or 200 to qualify. Unfortunately, Marion finished fifth in the 100 meters. In the 200 meters, she missed third place by seven one-hundredths of a second. The good news was that Marion was invited to join the 4 x 100 meters relay team as an alternate.

After talking it over with her mother, Marion made a startling decision. She informed the U.S. Olympic Committee that she would not attend the games. The American sprinters were almost guaranteed to win a gold medal in the relay, but it was unlikely that Marion would participate in more than one or two qualifying races. To stand in front of the world and accept a gold medal she had not earned seemed wrong to her. "I knew I wasn't going to get a chance to run in the final," she says. "When I get my first gold medal, I want to have sweated for it."

# Senior Sensation

chapter }

*"Give me three or four weeks with her, and she'll be jumping 23 or 24 feet."*

— **LONG-JUMP SUPERSTAR MIKE POWELL**

arion returned to Thousand Oaks for her senior year. Her performance for the basketball team was something special. She tore up the league, averaging 22.8 points and 14.7 rebounds a game. She was named California's top high school player.

During Marion's final track season at Thousand Oaks, she had little competition in the sprints. That is when she became interested in the long jump. It seemed natural to try it. She could run fast and jump high—could this be any more complicated? Marion soon discovered that it was. The long jump requires an athlete to be precise, then explosive, then creative—all in the span of a few precious seconds. Mess up any part of a jump and you have to junk it. The approach,

### Did You Know?

Marion was not only the best basketball player in California, in 1991, 1992, and 1993 but she was honored as the country's top schoolgirl track athlete.

*Marion won so easily and so often at Thousand Oaks that she decided to take up the long jump in her junior year.*

By 1993, Marion was the best schoolgirl long-jumper in California. What she lacked in technique she made up for with pure athletic ability.

the liftoff, and the midair mechanics must be blended perfectly, Marion found, or much of her power would go to waste. Often, she would charge down the runway so fast that it threw off the rest of her timing. Girls who could not stay close to Marion in a sprint sometimes outjumped her by a foot or more.

One of the few world-class sprinters who also mastered the long jump was Carl Lewis. He did so by actually *slowing down* his approach and concentrating mainly on his liftoff. Marion found this almost impossible—she knew of only one way to run, and that was as fast as she could. On those rare occasions when everything clicked, however, she achieved some eye-popping distances. At the 1993 California State High School Championships, Marion hit the pit at 22 feet $^1/_2$ inch to win the meet, coming up just 2 $^1/_2$ inches shy of the national schoolgirl record.

When it came time to choose a college, Marion decided to leave the West Coast, and also to focus on basketball. This broke the hearts of the coaches at California

*Marion knew the University of North Carolina was the right college the moment she set foot on campus.*

schools like UCLA and USC—and completely outraged people in the track world. They had always thought Marion was "theirs," and as she rose to national prominence, a lot of people in the sport hoped to become famous riding on Marion's "coattails." Marion, still fiercely independent, became uncomfortable with so many coaches and officials surrounding her all the time. So she decided to take a break. "I loved track and I wanted to keep it that way," she explains. "People in track tried to cling to me. I needed to get away from that."

Marion liked basketball because it was a team game. She eventually accepted a scholarship from the University of North Carolina. "It was my only official campus visit," she remembers. "I just fell in love with the school and the state. I walked down the street and people said hello to me. It was so different than California."

Marion's mother supported her decision. Carolina had a great communications and journalism department, an excellent record graduating minority students, and Marion was assured she could continue competing in track if she wanted. Marion also found UNC's basketball team very appealing. "I needed discipline," she admits, "and the Carolina basketball program is very structured."

## Did You Know?

When Marion enrolled at UNC, her mother moved with her to an apartment in Chapel Hill. It turned out to be a bad idea. The two Marions got on each other's nerves, and argued constantly. Big Marion finally moved out, but the damage was done—mother and daughter barely spoke for over a year.

# Getting to the Point

chapter 4

*"She looked at me
like I'd lost my mind."*
— **UNC COACH SYLVIA HATCHELL**

When Marion arrived at UNC, coach Sylvia Hatchell called her into her office. Marion, a high-scoring forward her entire basketball life, was told she would now be the team's backup point guard. Dismayed at first, Marion accepted this challenge and began to learn the skills her new position demanded. She came early to practice and stayed late,

*"The kid has focus like I've never seen, and I've worked with the Olympic team and All-Americans. She picked things up right away."*

SYLVIA HATCHELL

*Coach Hatchell gives team star Charlotte Smith a pep talk during the 1994 NCAA Tournament.*

working on her ball-handling and passing. Four games into her freshman season, Marion took over the starting job.

A fleet-footed point guard pressures the defense into mistakes. Marion, who possessed world-class sprinter's speed, created utter havoc. After a rebound, her teammates would fire the ball to her and she would streak down the court—often reaching the other basket before the defense had a chance to turn and set. Tar Heels opponents were so terrified of Marion's speed that often, when they missed a shot, they automatically turned and ran as fast as they could the other way. This made rebounding very easy for Carolina.

When the 1993–1994 season began, the experts ranked the Tar Heels around

10th in the country. By the end of the year, thanks to Marion and upper-classmen Tonya Sampson, Sylvia Crawley, and Charlotte Smith, Carolina had just two losses. Everyone was raving about Marion, even those who had criticized her for "turning her back" on track.

Despite their sparkling 27–2 record, the Tar Heels were still considered underdogs in the 1994 NCAA Tournament. Tennessee, led by Nikki McCray, and Connecticut, with "twin towers" Rebecca Lobo and Kara Wolters, looked unbeatable. But this was Carolina's year. Marion was on top of her game, Smith was shooting and rebounding like a monster, and Sampson was scoring at will.

One by one, UNC's opponents

*Sylvia Crawley, UNC's 6–5 center*

fell. In the opening round, the Tar Heels nearly doubled Georgia Southern's score, 101–53. Next, Old Dominion went down, 63–52. Vanderbilt, ranked above Carolina in the tournament seedings, lost by four, 73–69. Connecticut, a huge favorite, was humbled by Marion and company, 81–69. They forced the Huskies into making 30 turnovers, and Sampson scored 30 points against Lobo and Wolters. Purdue, an excellent team, failed to take the Tar Heels seriously. The Boilermakers clamped down on Sampson, so Marion kept feeding the ball to Smith, who scored 23 points in a 89–74 victory. And just like that, the Tar Heels found themselves in the NCAA championship game!

UNC's opponent in the final was Louisiana Tech, a school that had already won the national title twice. Like Carolina, however, Tech was a "Cinderella" team in this tournament. The Bulldogs had upset Mississippi, Tennessee, Southern California, and Alabama to reach the big game, and they too were on a roll.

*Charlotte Smith's fine shooting kept Carolina in the NCAA Final against Louisiana Tech— and eventually won it!*

The championship game was a tense, seesaw battle. Marion ran the floor like a whirlwind, and Smith ruled the boards with 23 rebounds. But in the final minutes, Tech's Pam Thomas scored 10 of her team's final 12 points, including a baseline jumper that gave the Bulldogs a 59–57 lead with just 15 seconds left. The Tar Heels came back down the court and Sampson fired up a 12-footer that clanked off the rim. A mad scramble ensued. Marion, one of the smallest players on the floor, used her speed to go after the rebound and grabbed the ball at the same time as a Tech player. The referee whistled a jump ball. Everyone in the Richmond Coliseum turned to see how much time was on the clock, and which way the possession arrow was pointing. It was Carolina's ball, but there was less than one second left in the game. Whoever got the ball for Carolina would have to catch and shoot in one motion—an impossible task.

Louisiana Tech coach Leon Barmore thought the Tar Heels would throw the ball to the 6–5 Crawley, and decided to double-team her. This allowed Stephanie Lawrence to inbound the ball without a defender in her face. Marion, Charlotte Smith, and Tonya Sampson raced around to get open. Crawley, already busy with two defenders, set a beautiful screen on a third Tech player to free up Smith, who sprinted toward Lawrence to receive the inbounds pass just beyond the three-point line.

As soon as the ball touched her fingers, it was on its way. Marion, standing open-mouthed at the foul line, watched along with a capacity crowd and a record television audience as, somehow, Smith's shot floated right into the basket. What had looked like a crushing, 59–57 defeat was transformed into a heart-stopping 60–59 victory. Marion and her teammates went bonkers. She had never felt this way before. They were national champions! It hardly seemed real.

No sooner had Marion finished celebrating UNC's national title than she found herself at the NCAA Track & Field Championships. Although she failed to win an event, Marion did well enough to earn All-America honors in four categories, including the long jump, in which she finished second. "It was a long basketball season," she says in her defense. "I had one and a half weeks of practice before the nationals."

*Somewhere in this pile is Marion Jones, the freshman point guard on the best team in the country.*

*Marion soars over a defender for an easy layup. Her quickness and leaping ability made her extremely hard to guard.*

chapter 5

# You Choose, You Lose

*"You don't put limits on what Marion Jones can do. In anything. Period."*

— **DENNIS CRADDOCK, UNC TRACK COACH**

arion continued to improve on the basketball court. She was named team co-captain and averaged 17.9 points and 4.8 assists as a sophomore. For the second year, she led the Tar Heels to the Atlantic Coast Conference (ACC) title. The team finished with a 30–5 record, but was eliminated by Stanford in the regional final of the 1995 NCAA Tournament.

Although track and field was no longer the focus of Marion's athletic career, she still competed and did well. After both her freshman and sophomore basketball seasons, she joined the Tar

*Marion's track coach, Dennis Craddock*

*Marion continued winning sprints in college, but her "basketball body" made it difficult to improve on her high-school times.*

Heel track squad in time for the ACC Championships. In 1994, Marion won the 100 meters and the long jump, placed second in the 200 meters, and was a member of Carolina's medal-winning 4 x 100 relay team. In 1995, she won the ACC long jump title again. Once more, Marion was invited to compete in the NCAA Track & Field Championships, where she finished fourth in the long jump and earned All-America honors again.

Most athletes would be pleased with these performances, especially since they came in a "second sport." But Marion felt she was going backward. Although she was winning events in college and making All-America teams, she had failed to improve on many of the personal bests she had established in high school. Marion knew what the problem was—the muscular upper body she had developed for basketball was not helping her as a sprinter, and it was weighing her down in the long jump.

With the 1996 Olympics little more than a year away, Marion had a decision to make. She believed she could make the U.S. basketball team, which was planning a long international tour prior to the Olympics. She also thought she could make the U.S. track team if she reshaped her body for her best events. That summer, Marion decided she would go for the gold in track. But first, she wanted to play basketball for Team USA in the World University Games.

This turned out to be a big mistake. During the tryouts, Marion broke a bone in her left ankle. This put her Olympic plans in jeopardy, because she would not have time to let the ankle heal and work her body into world-class form. Doctors told Marion her only choice was to have screws inserted in the bone. The ankle would be strong enough to let her begin her workouts after just a couple of months. Marion had the operation.

Part of Marion's training regime involved jumping on a trampoline. That winter, while bouncing, she landed awkwardly and bent the screws. Any hope of competing in the Olympics was now gone. Just as she had in 1992, Marion watched the games on television and was left to wonder what might have been.

Marion's ankle did heal in time for the 1996–1997 basketball season, which was a great relief to Coach Hatchell. During Marion's year off, the Tar Heels had flopped. Things got so bad that after the 1995–1996 regular season, Carolina was not even invited to participate in the 1996 NCAA Tournament.

Thanks to Marion, UNC was one of the top seeds in the 1997 NCAA Tournament. She had a sensational year, averaging 18.6 points and 4.1 assists, as the team went 29–3. In the tournament, however, the Tar Heels' luck ran out. After an impressive win against Harvard in the opening game, Carolina struggled to beat Michigan State in overtime. Against George Washington University in the third round, Marion and her teammates went ice cold in the final minutes and let the game slip away. It was a disappointing end to a great season. Little did anyone know, it would be Marion's last.

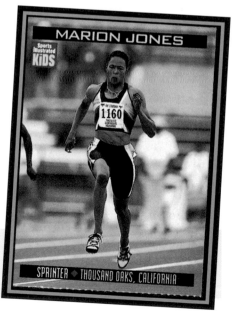

*Marion's trading cards
are the most collectible in her sport.*

*Marion felt good about the decision to "come back" to track.*

Technically, Marion Jones was eligible to play one more season of basketball for the University of North Carolina. The school had red-shirted her after her foot injury, so in basketball terms she still had her senior year. In the classroom, however, Marion had completed her senior year and was ready to graduate with a degree in journalism. Staying in school for the sake of playing ball seemed silly. Once again, Marion had to choose between basketball and track.

The success of the women's "Dream Team" at the 1996 Olympics had led to the creation of two professional leagues, the American Basketball League (ABL) and the Women's National Basketball Association (WNBA). Marion was told she could be a star in either league, and make a handsome living from hoops—something that seemed impossible just a few years earlier.

Funny, but the more Marion thought about basketball, the more she realized that she missed track. Having to watch the Olympic sprinters and long-jumpers from the sidelines the previous summer was one of the most difficult experiences of her life. Deep down Marion knew that, if she turned her back on the track world this time, she would be the one wondering why. "I loved my time at Carolina," Marion says. "And I loved playing basketball. I had four years to get an education and think about what I wanted to do with my life. I realized that what I wanted to do was track, which was always my first love."

That March, she informed Coach Hatchell of her decision, and began to prepare herself for her new career.

# Smart Switch

Marion's decision to return to track and field may go down as one of the smartest in sports history. No one doubts that she would have been a top player in the WNBA, but in track she has become a once-in-a-lifetime mega-star. Here is what the people who know Marion best have to say about her...

"Marion's a very fierce competitor, she has a perfect physique, and tremendous work ethic."
OLYMPIC TRACK COACH KAREN DENNIS

"Marion Jones is arguably the best athlete in the world right now."
CRAIG MASBACK USA TRACK & FIELD CEO

"I have been in Marion's shoes. It's just a matter of time before the world records come."
SUPERSTAR JACKIE JOYNER-KERSEE

"She's going to do some amazing things."
C.J. HUNTER

# Man With a Plan

chapter **6**

> *"In five minutes, Trevor showed her more than she'd learned in her whole life."*
>
> —C.J. HUNTER

When word spread that Marion was ready to reenter the track-and-field world, the reaction was a big yawn. The experts had seen this happen a hundred times before. Promising young athletes get lured into team sports in college all the time. When they decide to return to track, they discover that their bodies are "fighting" against them. In Marion's case, people assumed that the quickness she had developed as a point guard would rob her of her sprinter's speed, and the vertical leap she had practiced for basketball would keep her from exploding into her long jumps.

Marion knew she would encounter these problems, and often discussed her fears with her boyfriend, C.J. Hunter. A world-class shot-putter, C.J. first met Marion in 1995, while working as a strength coach for the Tar Heels track team. Right after

*World champion shot-putter C.J. Hunter has been #1 in Marion's
life since they met at the University of North Carolina in 1995.*

Marion decided to devote herself fully to track, C.J. introduced her to Trevor Graham, a former Olympian who had a reputation for unorthodox coaching methods. He remembered seeing her years before, in high school, and thinking she was special.

Graham watched Marion run a couple of times and could tell she still "had it." He made a few minor technical suggestions, and Marion could feel the difference immediately. "It was, like, automatic results," she marvels. "That had never happened to me."

Marion was excited. As they talked some more, she realized that Graham thought about sprints the same way she did.

*Marion strains to win at the 1997 World Track & Field Championships. She edged Zhanna Pintusevich (left) by .02 second to take home the gold in the 100 meters.*

Seven weeks after her final jump shot, Marion found herself at the U.S. Track & Field Championships with a new coach and a new attitude. Graham had taught Marion to stop thinking about races as explosions of energy. Instead, each sprint was a series of strides. By finding little ways to improve each stride, the time it takes to reach the finish line will go down dramatically. In Marion's case, she mostly needed to be more patient. "You can only run fast if you stay relaxed," she explains. "Tense up, and you can't attain a full range of motion."

When the heats for the 100-meter sprint began, no one paid much attention to Marion. But by the time the field had been whittled down and the participants in the final were determined, Marion had everyone leafing through the record books. In the semifinal heat, she had broken the tape in 10.92 sec-

Marion is still learning how to long jump. Although she has won many championships, she says she has yet to put together the "perfect" jump.

onds—one of the fastest times in history. In the final, Marion ignored the mind games the more experienced runners were trying to play and just focused on the 100 meters

"We all knew she was fast, but we also know it takes years to reach a high level. Everyone was shocked how quickly she hit those times."

INGER MILLER

ahead of her. She blew out of the starting blocks and won so easily that she actually *slowed up* at the end.

In the long jump, Marion went up against her idol, Jackie Joyner-Kersee, who had won this event the previous seven years in a row. After just a couple of jumps, it was clear that these two would be fighting it out for the gold medal. Marion took the lead, then Joyner-Kersee passed her in her final attempt, with a distance of 22 feet 8 inches. Unfazed, Marion responded with a jump of 22 feet 9 inches to win the event. Marion's two gold medals surprised the sports world. For a Division I basketball player to come out and blow away some of the best track-and-field athletes on the planet was hard to believe.

For the rest of the 1997 season, Marion proved she was for real. Gaining confidence and experience, and constantly fine-tuning her technique, she won two more gold medals at the World Championships in Greece—in the 100 meters and as part of the United States 4 x 100 relay team—and established herself as the woman to beat by smoking the sport's top sprinters throughout the summer track season.

At year's end, Marion was the number-one rated runner in the world at 100 and 200 meters, and was among the elite long jumpers. It seemed incredible, but Marion still had plenty of room left for improvement. Who could say what she might accomplish in 1998, when she would be fully focused on track?

Marion is considered tall for a sprinter. Here she towers over teammates
Gail Devers, Chryste Gaines, and Inger Miller after winning the
4 x 100 relay at the 1997 World Track & Field Championships.

# An Inch Short Of Perfect

# chapter 7

*"She's already recognized as one of the world's best, but she's really only starting to realize her potential."*

— CRAIG MASBACK, CEO OF
USA TRACK & FIELD

The dream of every athlete is to have a "perfect" season. In most sports this is impossible. A baseball player cannot get a hit every time he comes to the plate, a basketball player cannot make every shot, a tennis player cannot win every point, and a football player cannot score a touchdown every time he carries the ball. In track,

*Not since the days of superstar Edwin Moses has a track athlete had a year like Marion's 1998 season.*

perfection *is* possible. You can indeed win the final of every competition you enter. Edwin Moses, the great hurdler of the 1970s and 1980s, won 89 consecutive finals in the 400-meter hurdles, and had "perfect" years eight times.

Marion did not dare to dream such dreams. Her goals for 1998 were to do well again at the U.S. Track & Field Championships, win a couple of gold medals in the Goodwill Games, and finish the season on a strong note at the International Amateur Athletic Federation (IAAF) World Cup.

When the year was done, Marion had won the finals of every single race she entered! In all, she was unbeaten at four different distances in 1998: 60 meters, 100 meters, 200 meters, and also 400 meters—an event she had not entered since high school! Even when she was part of a relay team (when a teammate's mistake can lose a race) Marion did not lose.

## The Jones File

### MARION'S FAVORITE...

**Snack** . . . . . . . . . . . . . . . Licorice
**TV Show** . . . . . . . . . . . Judge Judy
**New Sport** . . . . . . . . . . . . . . Golf
**Saying** . . . . . . . "As long as you're running fast, life is good."
**Advice from Fans** . . . . . Give up the long jump. (It only makes her work harder.)

*After winning the 100 meters at the 1997 World Championships, Marion broke down in tears. "She started crying right away," remembers C.J. Hunter, her fiancé at the time. "It was quick, though. It's Marion. She even cries fast."*

At the U.S. Track & Field Championships, she became the first athlete in 50 years to win the 100 meters, 200 meters, and long jump. At the Goodwill Games, she took gold in the 100 and 200. At the Grand Prix Final, the year's top European event, she won the 100 meters and the long jump. And at the World Cup, Marion established new personal bests while winning the 100 meters (10.65 seconds) and 200 meters (21.62 seconds).

The only thing Marion lost in 1998 was her final competition of the season, the World Cup long jump. Until then, she was also perfect in this event. Whether she was

*Marion shows off two of the three gold medals she won at the 1998 U.S. Track & Field Championships. Her three golds marked the first time in 50 years that an athlete had accomplished this feat.*

exhausted from a long season or tentative on the rain-spattered track is hard to say, but Marion's attempt of 22 feet 11 ³/₄ inches fell just short of the winning jump, by German star Heike Drechsler. "I'm still thinking about that loss," admits Marion. "I couldn't get over that the season was over and there was no chance for redemption. She got the last say. That's the reason it really ate me up inside."

Fortunately, there was a silver lining in this lone dark cloud of 1998: Marion's second-place finish gave the United States team the overall championship by a razor-thin two points.

Best New Shoes: Find The Perfect Pair For You

World's Leading Running Magazine

SEPTEMBER 1998

RUNNER'S WORLD®

# Train Smart

How To:

- Reach Your Goals
- Visualize Success
- Prevent Shin Pain
- Stay Slim For Life
- Know Your Supplements
- Customize Your Workouts

Marion Jones
**America's Greatest Athlete**

$3.50US  $3.95CAN

0 74820 08665 0

www.runnersworld.com

*Runner's World proclaimed Marion "America's greatest athlete" in September 1998.*

*Marion beams after being presented with the Jesse Owens award for her incredible 1998 season.*

Marion ended the year as the world's top-ranked runner in the 100 and 200 meters, and she was the number-one long jumper. The only other woman in history to accomplish this was Irena Szewinska, the Russian star of the 1960s and 1970s. The only man to end a year rated first in these three events was Carl Lewis. When the time came to choose the sport's top athlete, the voting was not even close. Marion Jones, with her winning ways and unbeatable smile, was everyone's favorite. She won everything in sight that winter, including the prestigious Jesse Owens Award. The best part of the postseason, however, came in October. Marion and C.J. got married. It was a great ending to an incredible year.

*Track fans went searching for hard-to-find Irene Szewinska collectibles when they learned she was the only woman besides Marion to finish a year first in the 100, 200, and long jump.*

# C.J. and Me

The relationship between C.J. Hunter and Marion Jones has fascinated the track world since it began. To some they look like the ultimate odd couple—in magazine articles they are sometimes called "Beauty and the Beast." Others feel that they spend so much time together that it has hurt Marion's standing in the sport. Even Marion's mother was against their marriage. But those who knew Marion well way-back-when understand the important role C.J. has played in her life.

After suffering the injury that kept her out of the Olympics, Marion was extremely sad. Her sports career was in jeopardy, and her attempts to reach out to her father were unsuccessful. Around the time she and C.J. first met, in fact, she had just had a teardrop tattooed on her shoulder. C.J. was upbeat, fun, and caring—in other words, just what Marion needed. "He made me laugh," she remembers.

When UNC track coach Dennis Craddock heard about the budding romance, he informed C.J. of a university rule forbidding coaches and athletes to date. So C.J. quit his job. That impressed Marion. She had never had a boyfriend before, and no man (including her father) had ever shown her that kind of devotion.

For a time, Marion's coaches tried to talk her out of seeing C.J. They told her he was bad news, and that he had a reputation as a mean guy. Marion knew all about C.J.'s past, but she had her eye on the future. C.J. was bringing hope and order to her life. He helped Marion get a coach, and convinced Nike to sponsor her after she quit playing basketball.

Now Marion is a stepmother to the two children C.J. fathered in a previous marriage—a role she takes seriously and enjoys a lot. C.J. and Marion still spend almost all of their free time together. They even coach a youth league basketball team near their home in Apex, North Carolina. To those who still doubt the power of their relationship, they have two words: Who cares?

# Hard Target

# chapter 8

*"It's no walk in the park anymore. Everybody is right there, running fast."*

— **MARION JONES**

n 1997, Marion had "ambushed" her sport—no one saw her coming. In 1998, she had been the woman to beat in every event she entered, and obviously she responded to that challenge. The challenge for 1999 was a little more complicated. With the 2000 Olympics on the horizon, and only one major international event (the World Championships), Marion's task would be to find a balance between winning and preparing for the year ahead.

Is a long-jump record "in the cards" for Marion? Men's champion Mike Powell—who gives her pointers—thinks so. "She's amazing," he says. "I just hope I don't mess her up!"

*World Class Athletes*

*Marion finishes far ahead of Gail Devers to win gold in the 100 meters at the 1999 World Track & Field Championships.*

As she discovered, this could be tricky. The temptation for any athlete coming off of a history-making year is to try to repeat. The fans are paying a lot of money to see you break some records, and it is only natural to want to please them. You cannot afford to take it easy, because everyone else is trying to beat you. But you cannot push too hard, either. Finding this balance was impossible for Marion, who puts tremendous pressure on herself and has high expectations of her own ability. Going into the 1999 World Championships in Seville, Spain, she said she would like to win four—something no woman had ever done before.

Unfortunately, Marion fell short of this goal, winning just two medals and only one gold. In the 100 meters final, she just nipped Inger Miller at the tape, with an excellent time of 10.70. But in the long jump, she finished third, behind Spain's Niurka Montalvo and Italy's Fiona May. Though disappointed with her bronze medal, Marion

*Marion's twisted features tell a painful story, as she pulls up with back spasms in the 200-meter semifinals in Seville, Spain.*

told reporters she was satisfied that she had given it everything she had. She and Trevor Graham would simply have to work harder to improve her technique. Marion's fans still had hope she would win four golds. There was the 200 meters, plus two relay races left. If the U.S. coaches would let her compete in each, Marion could still do it.

Any thoughts of this happening ended the next day, when Marion came out of the turn in the 200 meters and then suddenly stopped, clutching her back and screaming in pain. The crowd at the Estadio Olympico grew hushed as Marion crumpled to the track,

*C.J. tries to comfort Marion as she is wheeled off the track. Back injuries are among the most painful in sports, but luckily Marion's was not considered serious.*

twisting in agony. She was rushed off on a stretcher, with C.J. at her side. Two hours later, she walked gingerly from the medical station to a waiting van and returned to her hotel. The good news was that the injury appeared to be back spasms, a muscular injury that usually is not serious. The bad news was that Marion would have to cancel the rest of her 1999 schedule.

That left the spring and early summer of 2000 to heal, fine-tune her body, and get in shape for the Olympics in Sydney. It was both the scariest and most exciting time of Marion's life—finally, after missing her chances in 1992 and 1996, she was going for the gold!

> ## Did You Know?
>
> Prior to her injury in Seville in 1999, Marion had won 21 consecutive finals in the 200 meters. She had not lost a race since 1997.

# Maybe the Greatest

## chapter 9

*"She's making the sport right now. She's showing the women you can be great. She's an inspiration."*

— **U.S. SPRINTER ZUNDA FEAGIN-ALEXANDER**

When Marion Jones made the decision to make track and field her full-time job, she had three goals: win five Olympic gold medals, break Florence Griffith Joyner's record for the 100 meters (10.49 seconds), and Galina Chistyakova's mark for the long jump (24 feet). With anyone else, you might be tempted to shake your head in disbelief. But with Marion, you get the feeling something historic could happen at any time. Indeed, by the time you read this, she may already have reached any or all of these goals!

Regardless of which records she breaks—or fails to break—Marion's contribution to her sport will live forever. For a brief time in the 1980s, sports fans were captivated by the exploits of tracks stars. But

> ## Did You Know?
> *Marion trains almost exclusively with male sprinters. They are the only ones who can give her a decent race!*

*Sprinter Kim Graham, who specializes in the 400 meters, is glad for the attention Marion has focused on women's track—and happy that Marion sticks to the 100- and 200-meter events!*

in the 1990s interest dropped off and the sport suffered. Marion changed all that. She not only made people want to attend track meets and watch them on television, but also made them afraid to turn away for fear they might miss something. As a result, millions of fans discovered the sport's other stars. As the 21st century begins, track and field is no longer buried in the back pages of the sports section. More often than not, it is front-page news.

Sprinter Kim Graham, who thanks her lucky stars that Marion only "dabbles" in her specialty (the 400 meters), said it best during Marion's wondrous 1998 season. "It's great to have someone like her in the sport," observed Graham. "People come to see her in action, then they learn who the other athletes are."

## Did You Know?

*One of Marion's big regrets is that she never met Florence Griffith Joyner, who died in her sleep in 1998.*

So is Marion the best track-and-field athlete ever? She says not yet. "I don't deserve the title right now—I still consider Jackie Joyner-Kersee the best female athlete and probably always will," she says. To be the best ever, claims Marion, "records will have to fall."

Not that they won't. Until the day she hangs up her spikes, Marion will never lose sight of what she wants to accomplish. "Before my career is over," she says, "I will attempt to run faster than any woman has ever run, and jump farther than any woman has ever jumped."

And then what? Look out, Chamique Holdsclaw! She'll probably want to play in the WNBA!

## Sprinting *Sensations*

*Marion's goal for the 2000 Olympics was to win five gold medals—in the 100, 200, and 400 meters, the long jump, and the 4 x 100 relay. Here are the all-time greats whose records she hoped to eclipse:*

| Athlete | Country | Olympics | Gold Medals |
|---|---|---|---|
| Jesse Owens | USA | 1936 | (4) 100, 200, 4 x 100 Relay, Long Jump |
| Fanny Blankers-Koen | Holland | 1948 | (4) 100, 200, 4 x 100 Relay, Hurdles |
| Bobby Morrow | USA | 1956 | (3) 100, 200, 4 x 100 Relay |
| Valerie Briscoe-Hooks | USA | 1984 | (3) 200, 400, 4 x 400 Relay |
| Carl Lewis | USA | 1984 | (4) 100, 200, 4 x 100 Relay, Long Jump |
| Florence Griffith Joyner | USA | 1988 | (3) 100, 200, 4 x 100 Relay |

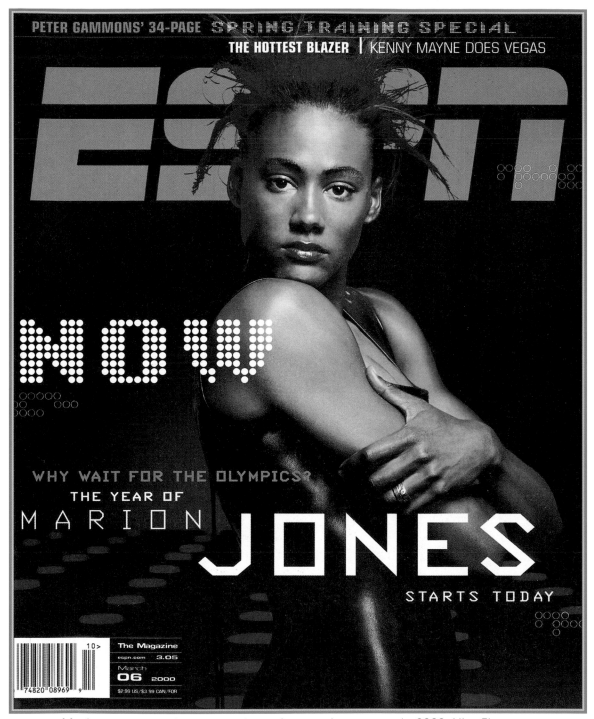

*Marion appeared on a number of magazine covers in 2000. Like Florence Griffith Joyner, she has captured the public's imagination and burst beyond the boundaries of her sport to become a true international celebrity.*

# Index

*PAGE NUMBERS IN ITALICS REFER TO ILLUSTRATIONS.*